THE SEASON FOR SINGING
American Christmas Songs and Carols

THE SEASON FOR SINGING

American Christmas Songs and Carols

Compiled by *John Langstaff*

With music harmonized and arranged by Seymour Barab
for piano or guitar accompaniment

Doubleday & Company, Inc.   Garden City, New York

The Carol of the Birds (Copyright 1943), I Wonder as I Wander (Copyright 1934), Sing We the Virgin Mary (Copyright 1942), and Jesus, Jesus, Rest Your Head (Copyright 1938), are reproduced by permission of G. Shirmer, Inc.

Library of Congress Cataloging in Publication Data

Langstaff, John M   comp.
　　The season for singing.
　　Illustrated by John Johnson
　　1. Christmas music. 2. Carols, English. I. Barab, Seymour, arr. II. John Johnson illus. III. Title.
M1629.3.C5L3　　783.6′55′2
Library of Congress Catalog Card Number 74-4064
ISBN 0-385-06564-7 Trade
ISBN 0-385-06566-3 Prebound

Introduction

The Christmas season is indeed a time for singing! At no other time of the year does music, particularly song, play such an important part in all that is going on. At family gatherings, parties, church and school performances we either participate and add our voices to the sound or we are bombarded on every side with "canned" familiar carols in the street, in stores, on radio and television.

It was not always thus. Many of our early colonial settlers were forbidden to celebrate Christmas with caroling. The real *carole* dance-song from earlier times had been driven underground by the Reformation and later by the Puritan suppression shortly before our country was settled. A hundred years later, by the time our country achieved independence, Christmas festivity and its special music were firmly established again in people's lives.

This collection is concerned with the American Christmas carol and song as it developed from those early years of our country, particularly stemming from traditional folk melodies, Afro-American song; and early hymn tunes. There has been no attempt to include the enormous output of more recently composed music for this season, as we feel that it is easily available.

The guitar chords suggested are not necessarily the same harmonies as those found in the piano accompaniment. For further simplification of guitar chords, alternate chords are occasionally given, as well as an indication for using the capo on a given fret, to facilitate fingering.

Contents

Shape-Note Hymns and Composed Songs

Part Songs

THE SEASON FOR SINGING
American Christmas Songs and Carols

FOLK CAROLS

Folk Carols

Remnants from antiquity can be found in some of the pure folk carols or traditional ballads of the United States. The widespread European narrative of Mary and Joseph in the orchard of cherries or apples goes back to the Apocrypha of the fifth century, in which the Virgin asks for dates from the palm tree. Our American version takes on its own homespun qualities and phrases. (There still are areas in our country where people celebrate Christmas on January 6, the date of "Old Christmas.")

The oldest manuscript of the "Seven Joys of Mary" is found in the British Museum and is from the fifteenth century, but we assume its origin in oral tradition may have been even earlier.

There are many charming Christmas songs from the Spanish-speaking Americans, particularly from Puerto Rico. We have given the original text and a freely adapted English version.

Christmas music for the most part is a Christian implantation on the cultures of the Eskimos, Hawaiians, and Indians. The one American Indian carol included here, beautiful though it is, is hardly representative of their authentic music but shows a probable influence of the Jesuit priests' teaching.

The Seven Joys of Mary

Appalachian mountain variant
collected by Richard Chase

With quiet movement

The__ first joy of Mar - y was the joy of one:

That the bless- ed Je - sus was born to be__ her son, Born to be__ her

son, O my Fa - ther in glo - ry, Born to be her son._____

The second joy of Mary was the joy of two,
    That her little Jesus could read the Bible through,
Read the Bible through, O my Father in glory,
    Read the Bible through.

The third joy of Mary was the joy of three,
    That her little Jesus could make the blind to see,
Make the blind to see, O my Father in glory,
    Make the blind to see.

The fourth joy of Mary was the joy of four,
    That her little Jesus could live for evermore,
Live for evermore, O my Father in glory,
    Live for evermore.

The fifth joy of Mary was the joy of five,
    That her little Jesus could bring the dead alive,
Bring the dead alive, O my Father in glory,
    Bring the dead alive.

The sixth joy of Mary was the joy of six,
    That her little Jesus could heal and cure the sick,
Heal and cure the sick, O my Father in glory,
    Heal and cure the sick.

The seventh joy of Mary was the joy of seven,
    That her little Jesus could turn the earth to heaven,
Turn the earth to heaven, O my Father in glory,
    Turn the earth to heaven.

Jesus Born in Bethlea

Traditional folk hymn
from Virginia

Down came an angel,
Down came an angel,
Down came an angel
To tell the world around,
To tell the world around,
To tell the world around.
Down came an angel
To tell the world around.

En el Portal de Belén (At the Crèche)

Traditional Puerto Rican
English adaptation by Seymour Barab

tar,   va - ya pro - si - go es - te can - tar.   Le - rum, le - rum, le - rum, la.___
bring - ing, all the world's here at Beth- le-hem's gate. Mer - ry Christ-mas one   and all!"___

En el portal da Belén	Round the stable angels hover
Hay estrella, sol y luna:	Kings and wisemen greet the child
La Virgen y San José	But to Mary and to Joseph
Y el Niño que está en la cuna.	Jesus gives his only smile.
REFRAIN	REFRAIN
Entró al portal un gallego	In the stable there's a shepherd
Que vengo desde Galicia	Linen cloth is all he brings;
Y le traigo al Niño Dios	It was meant to warm a baby,
Liesnzo para una camisa.	But it warms the King of kings.
REFRAIN	REFRAIN
Entró un gitano al partal	To the stable comes a gypsy
De Granada vengo a aquí	Full of wondering and fear;
Y le traigo al Niño Dios	As he gives the babe a rooster,
Un gallo quiquiriqui.	It crows out so loud and clear.
REFRAIN	REFRAIN

Sing We the Virgin Mary

Collected in Kentucky
and adapted by John Jacob Niles

So silent came our Jesus,
　Unto his sweet Mary,
As dew in April falleth
　On flow'r so tenderly,
On flow'r so tenderly.

When Jesus was a-borning,
　To earth came heaven down
To lie upon a manger
　Away in Beth'lem's town,
Away in Beth'lem's town.

So mirth ye well, all Christians,
   And sing in one accord;
Today in far off manger
   Mary hath birthed our Lord,
Mary hath birthed our Lord,

Los Reyes Oriente (Song of the Wise Men)

Traditional Puerto Rican
English adaptation by Seymour Barab

Moderately slow

(Capo III)

De tie-rra le-ja - na ve-ni-mos a ver-te
We have trav-elled far, all thought of rest for-sak-en,

nos sir-ve de guí - a la Es-tre-lla de O-rien-te.
Bid-den by a star to tread the path we've tak-en.

Refrain:

Oh bri-llan-te es-tre - lla que a-nun-cias la au-ro-ra
Bless-ed be this light that guides the a-lien stran-ger

no me fal-te nun - ca tu luz bien-he-cho-ra.
On this ho-ly night and leads him to the man-ger.

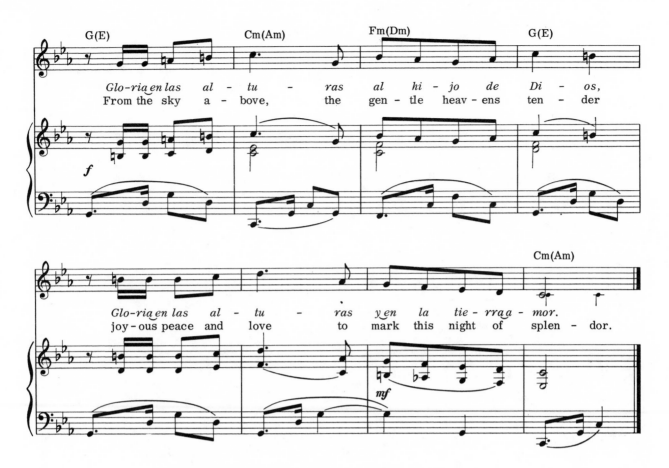

Al recién nacido, que es Rey de los reyes,
Oro le regalo para ornar sus sienes.

REFRAIN

Como es Dios el Niño le regalo incienso,
Perfume con alas que sube hasta el cielo.

REFRAIN

Al Niño del cielo que bajó a la tierra
Le regalo mirra que inspira tristeza.

REFRAIN

Golden gifts I bring to give him ease and pleasure,
As befits a king God gave the world to treasure.

REFRAIN

Frankincense I brought for when his prayers are given,
All their sweetness caught while drifting up to heaven.

REFRAIN

Bitter myrrh have I for tears the Good Lord gave us,
Men can never die while Jesus lives to save us.

REFRAIN

23

Hush, My Babe

Traditional tune from Tennessee
Words of Isaac Watts

As a lullaby

Hush, my babe, lie still and slum - ber; ho - ly an - gels guard thy bed.

Heav'n - ly bless - ings with - out num - ber gen - tly fall - ing on thy head.

Soft and easy is thy cradle;
Coarse and hard thy Savior lay,
When his birthplace was a stable
And his softest bed was hay.

I Saw Three Ships

Traditional variant from Virginia

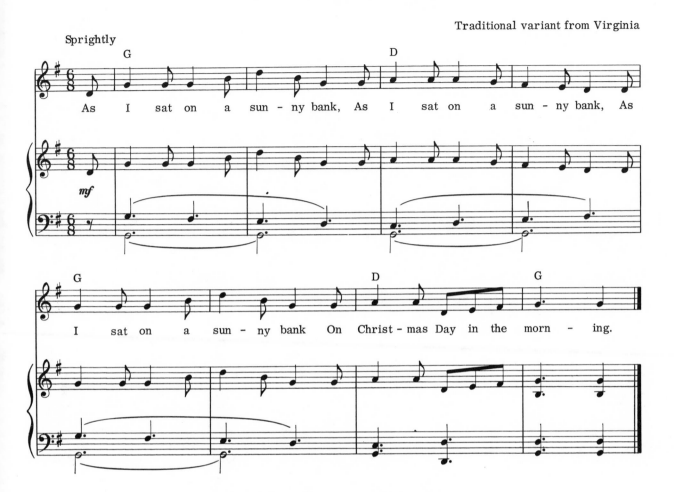

As I sat on a sun-ny bank, As I sat on a sun-ny bank, As I sat on a sun-ny bank On Christ-mas Day in the morn - ing.

I saw three ships come sailing by
   I saw three ships come sailing by
I saw three ships come sailing by
   On Christmas Day in the morning.

And who was in those ships all three
   And who was in those ships all three
And who was in those ships all three
   On Christmas Day in the morning?

'Twas Joseph and his fair lady
   'Twas Joseph and his fair lady
'Twas Joseph and his fair lady
   On Christmas Day in the morning.

Then he did whistle and she did sing
   Then he did whistle and she did sing
Then he did whistle and she did sing
   On Christmas Day in the morning.

And all the bells on earth shall ring
   And all the bells on earth shall ring
And all the bells on earth shall ring
   On Christmas Day in the morning.

The Cherry Tree Carol

Moving gently

Kentucky mountain ballad

(Capo V)

When Jo - seph was an old man, an old man was he, He court - ed Vir-gin Mar - y the Queen of Gal - i - lee, He court - ed Vir-gin Mar - y, the Queen of Gal - i - lee.

26

As Joseph and Mary,
 Were walking one day.
"Here are apples, here are cherries
 Enough to behold."
"Here are apples, here are cherries
 Enough to behold."

Then Mary spoke to Joseph
 So meek and so mild:
"Joseph, gather me some cherries,
 For I am with child."
"Joseph, gather me some cherries,
 For I am with child."

Then Joseph flew in anger,
 In anger flew he.
"Let the father of the baby
 Gather cherries for thee."
"Let the father of the baby
 Gather cherries for thee."

Then Jesus spoke a few words,
 A few words spoke he:
"Let my mother have some cherries,
 Bow low down, cherry tree."
"Let my mother have some cherries,
 Bow low down, cherry tree."

The cherry tree bowed low down,
 Bowed low down to the ground,
And Mary gathered cherries
 While Joseph stood around.
And Mary gathered cherries
 While Joseph stood around.

Then Joseph took Mary
 All on his right knee.
"What have I done, Lord?
 Have mercy on me."
"What have I done, Lord?
 Have mercy on me."

Then Joseph took Mary
 All on his left knee.
"Now tell me, little baby,
 When thy birthday will be."
"Now tell me, little baby,
 When thy birthday will be."

"On the sixth day of January
 My birthday will be,
When the stars and the elements
 Shall tremble with glee!"
When the stars and the elements
 Shall tremble with glee!"

Aguinaldo ("Mary," Said Saint Joseph)

Traditional Puerto Rican
English adaptation by Seymour Barab

With movement

Refrain: San Jo-séy_ Ma-rí-a van pa-ra_ Be-lén
"Mar-y" said_ Saint Jo-seph, "Can't we rest_ a-while?

San Jo-séy_ Ma-rí-a van pa-ra_ Be-lén
I am sore_ and wea-ry, walk-ing mile_ on mile."

Bus-can-do_ po-sa-da pa-ra nues-tro bién.
"Mar-y," said_ Saint Jo-seph, "Fear I'm grow-ing old.

Bus-can-do_ po-sa-da pa-ra nues-tro bién.
Nev-er felt_ so hun-gry, nev-er was_ this cold."

2. "Mary," said Saint Joseph,
    "What a trial it's been
    But the worst is over,
    Right ahead's an inn."

2. San José y María, (etc.)
    Aurora rosada
    de fresca color,
    puerto de los cielos,
    vos del Salvador.

Verses over

"Aguinaldo" continued

"Mary," said Saint Joseph,
"There we will be fed
They will build a fire,
We'll be warm in bed."

"No, my dearest husband,
Now my time has come
We must have a fire,
But to warm my son."

3. "Mary," said Saint Joseph,
"They sent me away
Said there was a stable
Only place to stay."

"Mary," said Saint Joseph,
"What do we do now?
You can't have your baby
Where they keep a cow."

"Yes, my dearest husband,
There's no time to spare
Take me to the stable
God is waiting there."

4. "Mary," said Saint Joseph,
"It's a little boy
Everyone is singing,
Singing out their joy.

"Mary," said Saint Joseph,
"Angels now appear,
Blessing this poor stable
And the child born here."

3. San José y María, (etc.)
Compiña morena
de hermoso matiz
se viste de flores
lozana y feliz.

4. San José y María, (etc.)
Anucian las aves,
al amanecer,
que vendrá del cielo
el Supremo Ser.

In the Valley

'Twas by his mother's hand
He was wrapped in swaddling band
And in a manger laid in the valley.

REFRAIN

SHAKER
MORAVIAN
INDIAN

Shaker, Moravian, Indian

The Moravians who had come from Europe to Pennsylvania established their communities with brass choirs and singing congregations, and their songs were principally in the form of anthems or hymns.

The Shakers of New York State and New England unknowingly may have come close to the feeling of the medieval *carole* in the simple steps and communal dance movement, combined with singing, which formed an important part of their worship. It is appropriate that we should include Sydney Carter's stirring contemporary text, "Lord of the Dance," which he has set to the Shakers' dancelike tune "Simple Gifts."

The Lord of the Dance

Shaker tune "Simple Gifts,"
with new words by Sydney Carter

I danced in the morn-ing when the world was be-gun, and I danced in the moon and the stars__ and the sun, and I came down from heav-en and I danced on the earth, at Beth - le - hem I had my birth. "Dance, then, wher - ev - er you may be, I am the Lord of the Dance," said he, "And I'll lead you all, wher -

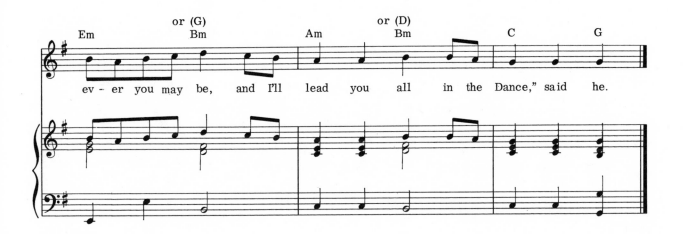

ev - er you may be, and I'll lead you all in the Dance," said he.

REFRAIN

"I danced for the scribe
And the pharisee,
But they would not dance
And they wouldn't follow me.
I danced for the fishermen,
For James and John,
They came with me
And the dance went on.

REFRAIN

"I danced on the Sabbath
And I cured the lame;
The holy people
Said it was a shame.
They whipped and they stripped
And they hung me on high,
And they left me there
On a Cross to die.

REFRAIN

"I danced on a Friday
When the sky turned black;
It's hard to dance
With the devil on your back.
They buried my body
And they thought I'd gone;
But I am the dance,
And I still go on.

REFRAIN

"They cut me down
And I leapt up high;
I am the life
That'll never, never die.
I'll live in you
If you'll live in me;
I am the Lord
Of the Dance," said he.

REFRAIN

The Huron Indian Carol

Quiet, noble

'Twas in the moon of win-ter-time when all the birds had fled, That might-y Gitch-i-man-i-tou sent an-gel choirs in-stead. Be-fore their light the stars grew dim and won-d'ring hunt-ers heard the hymn:— Je-sus, your king is born, Je-sus is born, in ex-cel-sis glo-ri-a.

Within a lodge of broken bark
    The tender babe was found,
A ragged robe of rabbit skin
    Enwrapped his beauty round.
The chiefs from far before him knelt
    With gifts of fox and beaver pelt.

REFRAIN

O children of the forest free,
    O sons of Manitou,
The Holy Child of earth and heav'n
    Is born today for you.
Come kneel before the radiant boy
    Who brings you beauty, peace and joy.

REFRAIN

Christ the Lord Most Glorious

John Antes (Moravian)
18th century

Christ The Lord, The Lord most glo - rious now is born, O shout a-

loud; Man by Him is made vic - to - rious. praise your Sav-ior, hail your God.

Praise the Lord, for on us shineth,
    Christ the Sun of righteousness;
He to us in love inclineth,
    Cheers our souls with joy and grace.

Praise the Lord, whose saving splendor
    Shines into the darkest night;
O what praises shall we render
    For this never-ceasing light!

Welcome Here!

Shaker "Welcome" song,
New York State

Strongly accented

Wel-come here, wel-come here, all be a-live and be of good cheer.

Wel-come here, wel-come here, all be a-live and be of good cheer.

Fine

Verse:

I've got a pie all baked com-plete,— pud-ding too, that's ver-y sweet.

Chest-nuts are roast-ing, join us here— While we dance and make good cheer.

D. C. al Fine

Verses over

41

"Welcome Here!" continued

I've got a log that's burning hot,
Toddy's bubbling in the pot.
Come in, ye people, where it's warm,
The wind blows sharp and it may storm.

REFRAIN

I made a loaf that's cooling there,
With my neighbors, I will share.
Come, all ye people, hear me sing
A song of friendly welcoming.

REFRAIN

BLACK TRADITION: SPIRITUALS AND GOSPEL

Black Tradition

The black tradition has developed a rich heritage of Christmas music, probably the largest store of indigenous Christmas music in the United States. Gospel and folk elements continue to provide variation and change to this day. Many of the spirituals have strong rhythmic forms. Their harmonies developed from Baptist hymns learned in the North and South.

Included is a variant of "Children, Go Where I Send Thee," which rivals in popularity the accumulative song, "The Twelve Days of Christmas."

The frequent use of choral refrain alternating with stanzas lined out by a leader provides us today with a form of song close to the *carole* of the Middle Ages.

Children, Go Where I Send Thee

Spirited

Black traditional carol

Chil-dren, go where I send thee. How will you send me?

I will send you one by one 'Cause one was the lit - tle bit - ty ba - by

- - cumulative repeat for subsequent verses - -

wrapped in the hol-low of a claw-horn, Ly - ing in a man - ger.

Born, Lord - y, Born in Beth-le - hem.

Children, go where I send thee.
    How will you send me?
I will send you two by two
    'Cause two was Paul and Silas,
One was the little bitty baby
    Wrapped in the hollow of a clawhorn,
Lying in a manger,
    Born! Lordy!
Born in Bethlehem.

. . . I will send you three by three
    'Cause three was the Hebrew children,
Two was Paul and Silas,
One was the little bitty baby, *etc*.

. . . I will send you four by four
    'Cause four was the four come a-knockin' at the door,
Three was the Hebrew children,
Two was Paul and Silas,
One was the little bitty baby, *etc*.

. . . I will send you five by five
    'Cause five was the gospel preachers,
Four was the four come a-knockin' at the door,
Three was the Hebrew children,
Two was Paul and Silas,
One was the little bitty baby, *etc*.

. . . I will send you six by six
    'Cause six was the six that couldn't get fixed,
Five was the gospel preachers,
Four was the four come a-knockin' at the door,
Three was the Hebrew children,
Two was Paul and Silas,
One was the little bitty baby, *etc*.

. . . I will send you seven by seven
    'Cause seven was the seven went up to heaven,
Six was the six that couldn't get fixed,
Five was the gospel preachers,
Four was the four come a-knockin' at the door,
Three was the Hebrew children,
Two was Paul and Silas,
One was the little bitty baby, *etc*.

. . . I will send you eight by eight
    'Cause eight was the eight that stood at the gate,
Seven was the seven went up to heaven,
Six was the six that couldn't get fixed,
Five was the gospel preachers,
Four was the four come a-knockin' at the door,
Three was the Hebrew children,
Two was Paul and Silas,
One was the little bitty baby, *etc*.

Verses over

47

♩..I will send you nine by nine
    'Cause nine was the nine got left behind,
Eight was the eight that stood at the gate,
Seven was the seven went up to heaven,
Six was the six that couldn't get fixed,
Five was the gospel preachers,
Four was the four come a-knockin' at the door,
Three was the Hebrew children,
Two was Paul and Silas,
One was the little bitty baby, *etc*.

. . . I will send you ten by ten
    'Cause ten was the ten commandments
Nine was the nine got left behind
Eight was the eight that stood at the gate
Seven was the seven went up to heaven
Six was the six that couldn't get fixed
Five was the gospel preachers
Four was the four come a-knockin' at the door
Three was the Hebrew children
Two was Paul and Silas
One was the little bitty baby, *etc*.

Rise Up Shepherd, and Follow

Music and Verses over

Rise Up, Shepherd, and Follow continued

If you take good heed to the angel's words,
   (Rise up, shepherd, and follow.)
You'll forget your flocks, you'll forget your herds.
   (Rise up, shepherd, and follow.)

REFRAIN

My Lord, What a Morning!

Spiritual

With intensity

(Capo V)

F(C)   B♭(F)   F(C)   Am(Em)   D(A)   Gm(Dm)   C(G)

My Lord, what a morn - ing! My Lord, what a morn - ing! Oh,__

F(C)   B♭(F)   F(C)   Gm(Dm)   Dm(Am)   C(G)   F(C)   *Fine*   Verse:

my Lord, what a morn - ing when the stars be - gin to fall.__ Oh, you will

Fine

C(G)   F(C)   B♭(F)   Gm(Dm)   C(G)

hear the trum-pet sound__ to wake the na - tions un - der - ground,

F(C)   B♭(F)   F(C)   Gm(Dm)   Dm(Am)   C(G)   F(C)   *D. C. al Fine*

Look-ing to my Lord's right hand when the stars be - gin to fall.

D. C. al Fine

Verses over

"My Lord, What a Morning" continued

REFRAIN

Oh, you will see my Jesus come,
His glory shining like the sun,
Looking to my Lord's right hand
When the stars begin to fall.

REFRAIN

Oh, you will hear all Christians shout,
'Cause there's a new day come about,
Looking to my Lord's right hand
When the stars begin to fall.

REFRAIN

Wasn't That a Mighty Day!

Spiritual

Moderate, with strong "gospel" beat

Was-n't that a might-y day, __ (Hal-le - lu, __ Hal-le - lu __)

Was-n't that a might-y day __ when Je - sus Christ was born. ___ Well,

Je - sus was a ba - by a - ly-ing at Mar - y's arm;

Ly-ing in the sta-ble at Beth-le - hem, __ the beasts, they keep-a him warm.

53

Mary Had a Baby

Traditional
From the Georgia Sea Islands

Mar-y had a ba-by, (Aye, Lord) Mar-y had a ba-by, (Aye, my Lord)

Mar-y had a ba-by, (Aye, Lord) The peo-ple keep a-com-ing and the train done gone.

Where did she lay him? (Aye, Lord)
Where did she lay him? (Aye, my Lord)
Where did she lay him? (Aye, Lord)
The people keep a-coming and the train done gone.

Laid him in a manger (Aye, Lord)
Laid him in a manger (Aye, my Lord)
Laid him in a manger (Aye, Lord)
The people keep a-coming and the train done gone.

What did she name him? (Aye, Lord)
What did she name him? (Aye, my Lord)
What did she name him? (Aye, Lord)
The people keep a-coming and the train done gone.

Named him King Jesus (Aye, Lord)
Named him King Jesus (Aye, my Lord)
Named him King Jesus (Aye, Lord)
The people keep a-coming and the train done gone.

Angels sang around him (Aye, Lord)
Angels sang around him (Aye, my Lord)
Angels sang around him (Aye, Lord)
The people keep a-coming and the train done gone.

Who heard the singin'? (Aye, Lord)
Who heard the singin'? (Aye, my Lord)
Who heard the singin'? (Aye, Lord)
The people keep a-coming and the train done gone.

Shepherds heard the singin' (Aye, Lord)
Shepherds heard the singin' (Aye, my Lord)
Shepherds heard the singin' (Aye, Lord)
The people keep a-coming and the train done gone.

Star kept a-shinin' (Aye, Lord)
Star kept a-shinin' (Aye, my Lord)
Star kept a-shinin' (Aye, Lord)
The people keep a-coming and the train done gone.

Oh Jerus'lem in the Morning!

Christmas Eve watch-night "shout"

Bright and spirited

Moth - er Mar - y, what is the mat - ter? (Oh, Je - ru - s'lem in the morn - ing!)

Fa - ther Jo - seph, what is the mat - ter? (Oh, Je - ru - s'lem in the morn - ing!) A

ba - by born to - day. ___ (Oh, Je - ru - s'lem in the morn ing!)

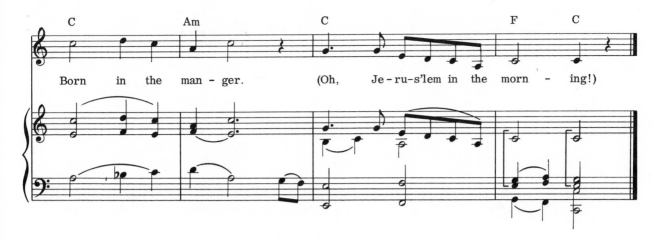

Born in the man - ger. (Oh, Je - ru - s'lem in the morn - ing!)

REFRAIN

Wrapped in swaddlin' clothes,
  (Oh, Jerus'lem in the morning!)
Stall was his cradle,
  (Oh, Jerus'lem in the morning!)

REFRAIN

Born in Bethlehem,
  (Oh, Jerus'lem in the morning!)
Baby born today,
  (Oh, Jerus'lem in the morning!)

Go, Tell It on the Mountain

Spiritual

Exultant

Go, tell it on the moun - tain, o-ver the hills and ev - 'ry-where!

Go, tell it on the moun - tain that Je - sus Christ is born! _____ While

Slower

shep-herds kept their watch - ing o'er si - lent flocks by night, Be-

hold, through-out the heav - ens, there shone a ho - ly light.

58

REFRAIN

The shepherds feared and trembled
When lo! above the earth
Rang out the angel chorus
That hailed our Jesus' birth.

REFRAIN

Down in a lonely manger
The humble Christ was born,
And God sent out salvation
That blessed Christmas morn.

REFRAIN

Poor Little Jesus

Spiritual from Louisiana,
Freely adapted by Seymour Barab

Poor little Jesus, (Yeah, Lord!)
He didn't have no cradle, (Yeah, Lord!)
They put him in a manger, (Yeah, Lord!)
They put him in a manger,
But from God he came;

REFRAIN

Poor little Jesus, (Yeah, Lord!)
His mother had to warm him, (Yeah, Lord!)
Of straw she made his blanket, (Yeah, Lord!)
Of straw she made his blanket,
But from God he came;

REFRAIN

Poor little Jesus, (Yeah, Lord!)
He should of had a cradle, (Yeah, Lord!)
He should of had a blanket, (Yeah, Lord!)
He should of had a blanket,
'Cause from God he came;

REFRAIN

Behold That Star

Spiritual

REFRAIN

The wise men came on from the East,
(This is the star of Bethlehem.)
To worship him, the Prince of Peace.
(This is the star of Bethlehem.)

REFRAIN

A song broke forth upon the night,
(This is the star of Bethlehem.)
From all the angels robed in white.
(This is the star of Bethlehem.)

REFRAIN

The Little Cradle Rocks Tonight

Spiritual from Georgia

The little cradle rocks tonight in glory,
Rocks in glory, rocks in glory,
The little cradle rocks tonight in glory,
The Christ child born in glory.

Peace on earth, Mary rock the cradle,
Rock the cradle, rock the cradle,
Peace on earth, Mary rock the cradle,
The Christ child born of glory.

The Christ child passing, singing softly.
Singing softly, singing softly,
The Christ child passing, singing softly,
The Christ child born in glory.

Sister Mary Had But One Child

Moderate

Spiritual

Refrain:

Sis - ter Mar - y had-a but one child,— born in Beth - le -
hem_____ And - a ev-er-y time - a the__ ba - by cried__ she - a
rocked him in the wea - ry land,_____ She - a rocked him in the wea - ry land.

Verse:

O three wise men__ to Je - ru-sa-lem came,__ they tra-velled-a ver - y far,__

Verses over

REFRAIN

An Angel appeared to Joseph,
And gave him this-a command,
"Arise ye, take your wife and child,
Go flee into Egypt's land.
For yonder comes old Herod,
A wicked man and bold,
He's slaying all the chillun
From six to eight days old."

REFRAIN

What You Gonna Call Yo' Pretty Little Baby?

verses over

"What You Gonna Call Yo' Pretty Little Baby" continued

What you gonna call yo' pretty little baby?
What you gonna call yo' pretty little baby?
What you gonna call yo' pretty little baby?
   Born, born in Bethlehem.
   Some call him one thing, I'll call him Jesus.
   Born, born in Bethlehem.

What you gonna call yo' pretty little baby?
What you gonna call yo' pretty little baby?
What you gonna call yo' pretty little baby?
   Born, born in Bethlehem.
   Sweet little baby, born in a manger.
   Born, born in Bethlehem.

SHAPE-NOTE HYMNS

COMPOSED SONGS

Shape Note and Composed Songs

Our first American composers wrote a number of splendid Christmas hymns, printed in the early shape-note song books and taught by itinerant music masters at singing schools throughout New England. These eighteenth-century composers were a vital part of their communities, as their trades show: tanners, farmers, circuit-rider preachers, blacksmiths, mathematicians, cabinetmakers, lawyers, coopers, and tavernkeepers. How often they were attracted to that part of the Nativity story concerning the shepherds out in the open fields, and how energetic and vigorous their music in setting those naïve texts!

By the beginning of the nineteenth-century, the fervent camp meeting and revivalist movements were spreading across the country to the West and South. Folk songs were often the music to which sacred hymn texts were matched, and we find many examples today of these traditional tunes in the white spirituals from that time (i.e., "Babe of Bethlehem").

We often forget that some of the best known Christmas hymns are American in origin. "It Came Upon the Midnight Clear" was written by a minister in Wayland, Massachusetts; Boston's great preacher Phillips Brooks wrote the words to "O Little Town of Bethlehem" when he was at a parish in Philadelphia; and "We Three Kings of Orient Are" was written by a rector in Williamsport, all in the 1800's.

The Babe of Bethlehem

Folk hymn from
Southern Harmony shape-note hymnal

Ye na-tions all,__ on ye I call, come hear this dec-la-ra-tion, And

don't re-fuse__ this glo-rious news of Je-sus and__ sal-va-tion. To

roy-al__ Jews came first the__news of Christ, the great__ Mes-si-ah, As

'twas fore-told__ by proph-ets old, I-sai-ah, Je-re-mi-ah.

To Abraham the promise came and to his seed forever,
    A light to shine in Isaac's line, by Scripture we discover;
Hail promised morn the Saviour's born, the glorious Mediator.
    God's blessed Word made flesh and blood, assumed the human nature.

His parents poor in earthly store, to entertain the stranger
    They found no bed to lay his head, but in the ox's manger:
No royal things as used by kings, were seen by those that found him.
    But in the hay the stranger lay, with swaddling bands around him.

On that same night a glorious light to shepherds there appearéd,
    Bright angels came in shining flame, they saw and greatly fearéd.
The angels said, "Be not afraid, although we much alarm you,
    We do appear good news to bear, as now we will inform you."

Then with delight they took their flight, and winged their way to glory,
    The shepherds gazed and were amazed, to hear the pleasing story;
To Bethlehem they quickly came, the glorious news to carry,
    And in the stall they found them all, Joseph, the Babe and Mary.

The shepherds then returned again to their own habitation,
    With joy of heart they did depart, now they have found salvation;
"Glory," they cry, "to God on high, who sent his Son to save us!
    This glorious morn the Saviour's born, his name it is Christ Jesus."

"The city's name is Bethlehem, in which God hath appointed,
    This glorious morn a Saviour's born, for him hath God anointed;
By this you'll know: if you will go, to see this little Stranger,
    His lovely charms in Mary's arms, both lying in a manger."

When this was said, straightway was made a glorious sound from heaven:
    Each flaming tongue an anthem sung, "To men a Saviour's given,
In Jesus' name, the glorious theme, we elevate our voices
    At Jesus' birth, be peace on earth, meanwhile all heav'n rejoices."

Wondrous Love

Ye wingéd seraphs fly,
　　Bear the news, bear the news!
Ye wingéd seraphs fly,
　　Bear the news!
Ye wingéd seraphs fly,
　　Like angels in the sky,
Fill vast eternity
With the news, with the news.
Fill vast eternity
With the news.

To God and to the Lamb,
　　I will sing, I will sing.
To God and to the Lamb,
　　I will sing.
To God and to the Lamb,
　　Who is the great I Am,
While millions join the theme
I'll sing on, I'll sing on.
While millions join the theme
I'll sing on.

Star in the East

A Southern shape-note hymn

Hail, bless-ed morn!_ See the Great Me-di-a-tor down from the re-gions of Glo-ry de-scend! Shep-herds, go wor-ship the babe in the man-ger, Lo, for a guard_ the bright an-gels at-tend. Bright-est and best of the sons of the morn-ing, dawn on our dark-ness and lend us Thine aid:

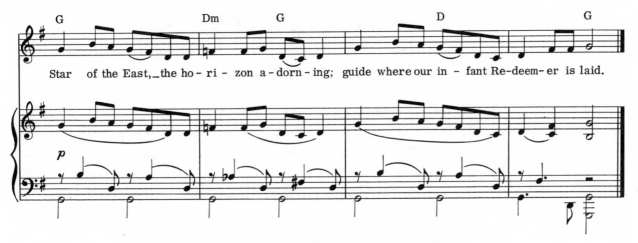

Star of the East,__the ho - ri - zon a - dorn - ing; guide where our in - fant Re-deem- er is laid.

Cold on his cradle the dew-drops are shining,
    Low lies his head with the beasts of the stall;
Angels adore him in slumber reclining,
    Maker and monarch and Saviour of all.

REFRAIN

Shall we not yield him in costly devotion,
    Odors of Edom, and offerings divine,
Gems of the mountain and pearls of the ocean,
    Myrrh from the forest, and gold from the mine?

REFRAIN

Vainly we offer each ample oblation,
    Vainly with gifts would his favor secure;
Richer by far is the heart's adoration,
    Dearer to God are the prayers of the poor.

REFRAIN

While Shepherds Watched

Jubilant

Shape-note hymn

While shep - herds watched___ their___ flocks by___ night, all seat - ed on___ the ground, the an - gel of_____ the Lord___ came down___ and glo - ry shone_ a - round. The an - gel of the_ Lord_ came_ down, and glo - ry shone a - round, The an - gel of the

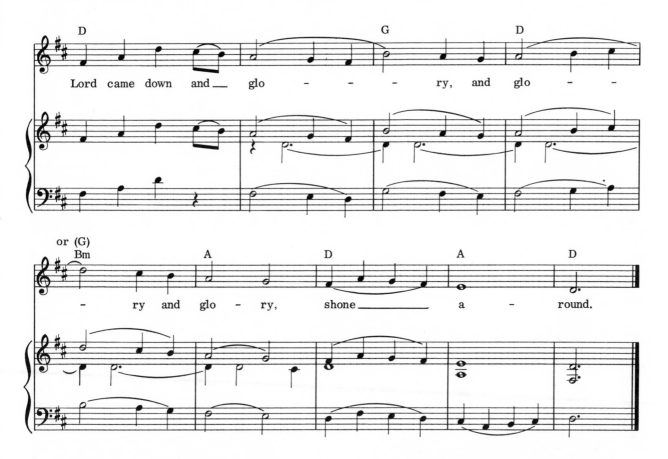

Lord came down and glo - - - ry, and glo - - - ry and glo - ry, shone a - round.

"Fear not," said he (for mighty dread
    Had seized their troubled mind);
"Glad tidings of great joy I bring
    To you and all mankind,
"Glad tidings of great joy I bring
    To you and all mankind,
Glad tidings of great joy I bring
    To you, to you and all mankind."

"To you in David's town this day
    Is born of David's line
A Saviour, who is Christ the Lord;
    And this shall be the sign:
    etc.

"The Heavenly Babe you there shall find
    To human view displayed
All meanly wrapped in swathing bands,
    And in a manger laid,
    etc.

Thus spake the Seraph; and forthwith
    Appeared a shining throng
Of angels praising God, who thus
    Addressed their joyful song:
    etc.

"All glory be to God on high,
    And to the earth be peace;
Good-will henceforth from heaven to men
    Begin and never cease,
    etc.

All Hail to the Morning

Anonymous Pennsylvania hymn, 1840,
Words of Samuel Wakerfield

In - fant Re - deem - er is laid. Go, shep - herds and vis - it the
won - der - ful stran - ger! Let acts of de - vo - tion un - to him be paid.

Exultation

From Southern harmony shape-note hymnal

With a quick, strong beat

Come a-way to the skies,— my be-lov-ed, a-rise and re-joice in the day— thou wast born;——— On this fest-i-val day, come ex-ult-ing a-way and with sing-ing to Zi-on re-turn.———

There, oh there, at his feet we shall all likewise meet
And be parted in body no more.
We shall sing to our lyres with heavenly choirs,
And our Saviour in glory adore.

Now with singing and praise let us spend all our days
By our heavenly Father bestowed;
While his grace we receive from his bounty, and live
To the honor and glory of God.

Away in a Manger

Anonymous, published by
the Evangelical Lutheran Church, 1885

The cattle are lowing, the poor baby wakes,
But little Lord Jesus no crying he makes.
I love thee, Lord Jesus, look down from the sky
And stay by my cradle till morning is nigh.

Jesus, Jesus, Rest Your Head

John Jacob Niles

Je-sus, Je-sus, rest your head, you has got a man-ger bed:

All the e - vil folks on earth sleep in feath - ers at their_ birth,

Je-sus, Je-sus, rest your head, you has got a man-ger bed.

Verse: Have you heard a - bout our Je - sus, have you heard a - bout his fate?

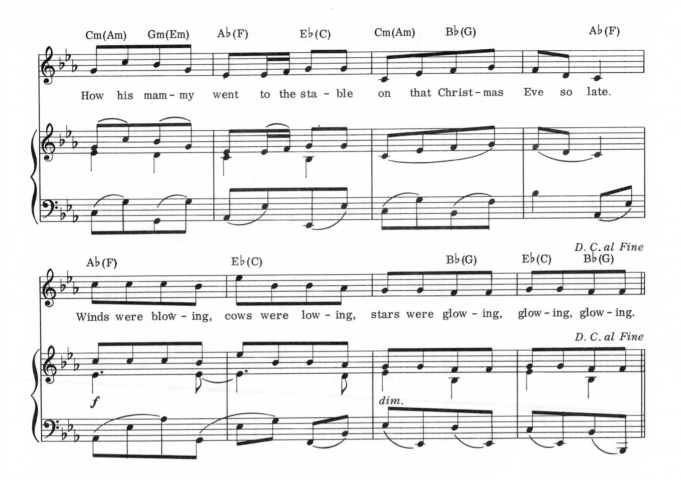

How his mam-my went to the sta-ble on that Christ-mas Eve so late.

Winds were blow-ing, cows were low-ing, stars were glow-ing, glow-ing, glow-ing.

D. C. al Fine

To that manger came then wisemen,
    Bringing things from hin and yon
For the mother and the father
    And the blesséd little son.
Milk-maids left their fields and flocks
    And sat beside the ass and ox.

REFRAIN

A Virgin Unspotted

William Billings,
from The Singing Master's Assistant, 1778

A Vir-gin un-spot-ted, ye Proph-et fore-told, should bring forth a Sav-iour, which now we be-hold, to be our Re-deem-er from death, hell and sin, which Ad-am's trans-gres-sion in-vol-véd us in. Then— let us be— mer-ry, put sor-row a-way, our Sav-iour, Christ Je-sus was born on this day. Then—

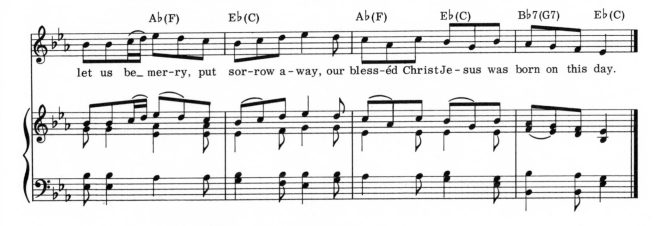

let us be_ mer-ry, put sor-row a-way, our bless-éd Christ Je-sus was born on this day.

In Bethlehem city in Jud'a it was
That Joseph and Mary together did pass,
All for to be taxéd when thither they came
Since Caesar Augustus commanded the same.

REFRAIN

Now Mary's full time being come, as we find,
She brought forth her first born to save all mankind,
The inn being full for this heavenly guest,
No place there was found for to lay him to rest.

REFRAIN

But Mary, blest Mary, so meek and so mild,
Soon wrapt up in swaddling this heavenly child.
Contented she laid him where oxen do feed;
The great God of nature approved of the deed.

REFRAIN

God sent down an angel from heaven on high,
To certain poor shepherds in fields as they lie,
And made them no longer in sorrow to stay,
Because that our Saviour was born on this day.

REFRAIN

Then presently after the shepherds did spy
Vast numbers of angels to stand in the sky;
So merrily talking, so sweet they did sing,
All glory and praise to our heavenly King.

REFRAIN

I Wonder as I Wander

Freely expressive

John Jacob Niles

*Dm7

When Mary birthed Jesus, 'twas in a cow's stall
With wise men and farmers and shepherds and all.
But high from God's heaven a star's light did fall,
And the promise of ages it did then recall.

If Jesus had wanted for any wee thing,
A star in the sky, or a bird on the wing,
Or all of God's angels in heaven for to sing,
He surely could have it, 'cause He was the King.

I wonder as I wander, out under the sky,
How Jesus the Savior did come for to die
For poor or'n'ry people like you and like I;
I wonder as I wander, out under the sky.

Shepherds in Judea

Jeremiah Ingalls,
New Hampshire, 1805

As shep - herds in Jew - ry were guard - ing their sheep, Pro -
mis - c'ous-ly seat - ed, es - trang - éd from sleep, An an - gel from
heav - en pre-sent - ed to view And thus__ he ac - cost - ed the
trem - bl - ing few: "Dis - pel all your sor-rows and ban-ish your fears, For__

Je - sus, your Sav - iour, in Jew - ry ap - pears. Dis - pel all your sor - rows and

ban - ish your fears, For Je - sus, your Sav - iour, in Jew - ry ap - pears."

As shepherds in Jewry were guarding their sheep,
Promiscuously seated, estranged from sleep,
An angel from heaven presented to view,
And thus he accosted the trembling few:
    Dispel all your sorrows and banish your fears,
    For Jesus your Savior in Jewry appears.
    Dispel all your sorrows and banish your fears,
    For Jesus your Savior in Jewry appears.

A token I leave you, whereby you may find
This heavenly stranger, this friend to mankind:
A manger his cradle, a stall his abode,
The oxen are near him and blow on your God.
    Then shepherds be tranquil, this instant arise,
    Go visit your Savior and see where he lies.
    Then shepherds be tranquil, this instant arise,
    Go visit your Savior and see where he lies.

This wonderful story scarce reachéd the ear,
When thousands of angels in glory appear,
They join in the concert, and this was the theme:
All glory to God, and good will towards men.
    Then shepherds, go join your glad voice to the choir
    And catch a few sparks of celestial fire.
    Then shepherds, go join your glad voice to the choir
    And catch a few sparks of celestial fire.

verses over

93

Hosanna! the angels in ecstasy cry,
Hosanna! the wandering shepherds reply;
Salvation, redemption are center'd in one,
All glory to God for the birth of his Son.
    Then shepherds, adore, we commend you to God.
    Go visit the Son in his humble abode.
    Then shepherds, adore, we commend you to God.
    Go visit the Son in his humble abode.

To Bethlehem city the shepherds repair'd,
For full confirmation of what they had heard;
They enter'd the stable, with aspect so mild,
And there they beheld the Mother and Child.
    Then shepherds, be humble, be meek and be low,
    For Jesus your Savior's abundantly so.
    Then shepherds, be humble, be meek and be low,
    For Jesus your Savior's abundantly so.

The Season for Singing

Words and Music by
Seymour Barab

The sea-son for sing-ing a joy-ous re-frain has come to all men of good
will once a-gain; Let voic-es u-nite in har-mo-nious ac-cord to
tell of the glo-ri-ous birth of our Lord.

We sing of the manger in which he was laid,
Of Joseph and Mary, the journey they made;
We sing of the shepherds, the vigil they kept,
And angels who blessed the small babe as he slept.

The tale that we sing has for ages been told,
It's grandeur and beauty can never grow old;
The season has music for all of the earth
Recalling the joy of our Lord's holy birth.

The Carol of the Birds

John Jacob Niles

The lark, the dove, the red bird came,
    Curoo, curoo, curoo,
The lark, the dove, the red bird came
    And worshipped there in Jesus' name,
On Christmas day in the morning,
    Curoo, curoo, curoo,
Curoo, curoo, curoo.

The owl was there, his eyes so wide,
    Curoo, curoo, curoo,
The owl was there, his eyes so wide
    As he did sit at Mary's side,
On Christmas day in the morning,
    Curoo, curoo, curoo,
Curoo, curoo, curoo.

We Three Kings

Like a processional

John Henry Hopkins, 1857

We three kings of O - ri - ent are; Bear - ing gifts we tra-verse a -

far. Field and foun - tain, moor and moun - tain, fol - low - ing yon - der star.

O, — star of won - der, star of night, star with roy - al beau - ty bright,

West - ward lead - ing, still pro - ceed - ing, guide us to thy per - fect light.

Melchior Born a king on Bethlehem's plain,
Gold I bring, to crown him again,
King forever, ceasing never,
Over us all to reign.

REFRAIN

Caspar Frankincense to offer have I,
Incense owns a Deity nigh,
Prayer and praising, all men raising,
Worship him, God most High.

REFRAIN

Balthazar Myrrh is mine, its bitter perfume
Breathes a life of gathering gloom;
Sorrowing, sighing, bleeding, dying,
Sealed in the stone-cold tomb.

REFRAIN

Glorious, now, behold him arise,
King and God and Sacrifice,
Alleluia, Alleluia;
Earth to heaven replies.

REFRAIN

O Little Town of Bethlehem

Music by Lewis H. Redner
Words by Phillips Brooks

For Christ is born of Mary
   And gathered all above,
While mortals sleep,
   The angels keep
Their watch of wondering love.
   O morning starts together
Proclaim the holy birth,
   And praises sing to God the King
And peace to men on earth.

How silently, how silently,
   The wondrous gift is given!
So God imparts to human hearts
   The blessings of His heaven.
No ear may hear His coming,
   But in this world of sin
Where meek souls will receive Him still,
   The dear Christ enters in.

O holy Child of Bethlehem!
   Descend to us, we pray;
Cast out our sin, and enter in,
   Be born in us today!
We hear the Christmas angels
   The great glad tidings tell,
O come to us, abide with us,
   Our Lord Immanuel!

It Came upon a Midnight Clear

Music by Richard Storrs Willis
Words by Edmond H. Sears, 1850

It came up-on— a mid-night clear, that glo-rious song— of old,—— From an-gels bend-ing near the earth to touch their harps— of gold:—— "Peace on the earth,— good will to men, from heav'n's— all-gra-cious King."—— The world in sol-emn still-ness lay to hear the an-gels sing.——

Still through the cloven skies they come
    With peaceful wings unfurled,
And still their heav'nly music floats
    O'er all the weary world;
Above its sad and lowly plains
    They bend on hov'ring wing,
And ever o'er its Babel sounds
    The blessed angels sing.

For lo! the days are hastening on,
    By prophets seen of old,
When with the ever circling years,
    Shall come the time foretold,
When the new heaven and earth shall own
    The Prince of Peace their King;
And the whole world send back the song
    Which now the angels sing.

PART SONGS

Part Songs

For group singing in parts we have included some three- and four-part arrangements of a few songs from this collection, as well as several seasonal rounds. Notice that in some of these settings the melody does not necessarily lie in the top voice throughout.

Rounds are a simple way of singing in harmony. We include two of the earliest ones composed in colonial America and one written in New York City a month ago. Sing through the entire round in unison first, so that the tune is well established, before dividing into separate parts to follow one another. A decision has to be made as to how the round will finish. After singing the round through a number of times, an ending can be made by all parts simultaneously pausing on the final note of whichever phrase they are singing at that moment, thus creating a chord; or each part can gradually drop out as it reaches the very end of the round's melody.

Sing We the Virgin Mary

Traditional folk song
Arranged for three parts
by Seymour Barab

Sing we the Vir-gin Mar - y, sing we that match-less one; See how the an - gels at-tend - ed her when she birth- éd God's own son, When she birth- éd God's own son.

Wake Ev'ry Breath

Canon for six voices
by William Billings

With elation

1. Wake ev - 'ry breath ___ and ev - 'ry string.

2. To bless the great ___ Re - deem - er King,

3. His name thro' ev - 'ry clime ___ a - dor'd:

4. Let joy ___ and grat - i - tude ___ and ___ love, ___

5. Thro' all ___ the notes ___ of mu - sic ___ rove; ___

6. And Je - - sus sound ___ on ev - 'ry ___ chord.

rehearsal only

Behold That Star

was no room found at the inn.__ (This is the star of Beth-le-hem.)__ For

was no__room found at the inn. (This is the star of Beth-le-hem.)__ For__

was no room found at the inn._____ (This is__ the star of Beth-le-hem.)__ For__

was no__room found at the inn. (This is__ the star of Beth-le-hem.)__ For

him who was born free from sin.__ (This is the star of Beth-le-hem.)__

him__who__was__born free from sin. (This is the star of Beth-le-hem.)__

him__who__was__born free from sin._____ (This is__ the star of Beth-le-hem.)__

him who was born__free from sin. (This is__ the star of Beth-le-hem.)__

When Jesus Wept

Canon for four voices
by William Billings

Hush, My Babe

Tennessee folk tune
Arranged for female voices
by Seymour Barab

Jesus Born in Bethlea

Folk hymn
Arranged for mixed voices
by Seymour Barab

114

in the man - ger lay, _____ and in the man - ger lay.

in the man - ger lay, _____ and in the man - ger lay. _____

in the man - ger lay, _____ and in the man - ger lay. _____

in the man - ger lay, _____ and in the man - ger lay.

Je - sus born in Beth - lea and in the man - ger lay.

Je - sus born in Beth - lea, and in the man - ger lay.

Je - sus born in Beth - lea, and in the man - ger lay.

Je - sus born in Beth - lea, and in the man - ger lay.

The Seven Joys of Mary

Traditional folk carol
Arranged for three parts
by Seymour Barab

son, O my Fa - ther in glo - ry, born to be her son.___

be her son, O glo - ry, born to be her son, her__ son.

be her son, O glo - ry, born to be her son.___

Christ the Lord Most Glorious

Moravian tune by John Antes
Arranged for four parts
by Seymour Barab

Star of Bethlehem

Canon in three parts
by Louis Haber
Words by Seymour Barab

Quietly

1. See the Star of Beth - le - hem, where it leads we fol - low;

2. See the Star of Beth - le - hem, where it leads we fol -

3. See the Star of Beth - le - hem, where it leads we

now is born the king of men, where he leads we fol - low.

low; now is born the king of men, where he leads we fol - low.

fol - low; now is born the king of men, where he leads we fol - low.

One of America's leading concert artists, **John Langstaff** is the author of a number of books for children. He hosted the NBC series "Children Explore Books," soloist in the 1966 NBC Christmas special "A Christmas Masque" (shown nationwide), anchor man for the BBC TV series "Making Music," and twenty-five original programs for introducing and teaching music for WNET Channel 13, New York. He was host and narrator of "The Lively Art of Picture Books." He has directed and mounted a number of operas for children.

Seymour Barab started his musical career at the age of thirteen as the organist of a church in Chicago. A gifted cellist who has been a member of some of the country's outstanding orchestras, he is gaining a reputation as a composer. His music, widely performed, runs the gamut from grand opera (for which he is his own librettist) to popular song.

Index of First Lines

part song version